MEASURING AND COMPARING

How Heavy is Heavy?

Comparing Vehicles

Vic Parker

www.raintreepublishers.co.uk
Visit our website to find out more information about Raintree books.

To order:
☎ Phone 0845 6044371
🖷 Fax +44 (0) 1865 312263
🖳 Email myorders@raintreepublishers.co.uk

Customers from outside the UK please telephone +44 1865 312262

Raintree is an imprint of Capstone Global Library Limited, a company incorporated in England and Wales having its registered office at 7 Pilgrim Street, London, EC4V 6LB – Registered company number: 6695582

Edited by Nancy Dickmann, Rebecca Rissman, and Sian Smith
Designed by Victoria Allen
Picture research by Hannah Taylor
Original illustrations © Capstone Global Library Ltd
Original illustrations by Victoria Allen
Production by Victoria Fitzgerald
Originated by Dot Gradations Ltd
Printed and bound in China by South China Printing Company Ltd

ISBN 978 0 431 00621 5 (hardback)
14 13 12 11 10
10 9 8 7 6 5 4 3 2 1

ISBN 978 1 406 21952 4 (paperback)
15 14 13 12 11
10 9 8 7 6 5 4 3 2 1

British Library Cataloguing in Publication Data

Parker, Victoria.
How heavy is heavy? : comparing vehicles. --
(Measuring and comparing)
1. Weight (Physics)--Measurement--Juvenile literature.
I. Title II. Series
530.8-dc22

Acknowledgements
The author and publisher are grateful to the following for permission to reproduce copyright material: Alamy Images pp.**9** (© www.gerardbrown.co.uk), **12** (© John Warburton-Lee Photography), **14** (© Mark Scheuern); © Capstone Publishers pp.**4**, **6**, **26**, **27** (Karon Dubke); istockphoto p.**8** (© Hafizov Ivan); Photolibrary pp.**5** (Hill Street Studio), **10** (Frank Siteman), **16** (Chad Ehlers), **18** (Keith Levit Photography), **20** (Horst Mahr), **24** (Tsuneo Nakamura); shutterstock p.**22** (MarchCattle); Wayne Howes p.**25**.

Photographs used to create silhouettes: istockphoto, hot air balloon (© Elaine Barker), scales; shutterstock, toy scooter (© Korybolga), mountain bike (© Polina Katritch), Mini (© faberfoto), fire engine (© scoutingstock).

Cover photograph of a large truck transporting iron ore reproduced with permission of shutterstock (© SergioZ).

Every effort has been made to contact copyright holders of material reproduced in this book. Any omissions will be rectified in subsequent printings if notice is given to the publisher.

Disclaimer

MEASURING AND COMPARING

How Heavy is Heavy?

COMPARING VEHICLES

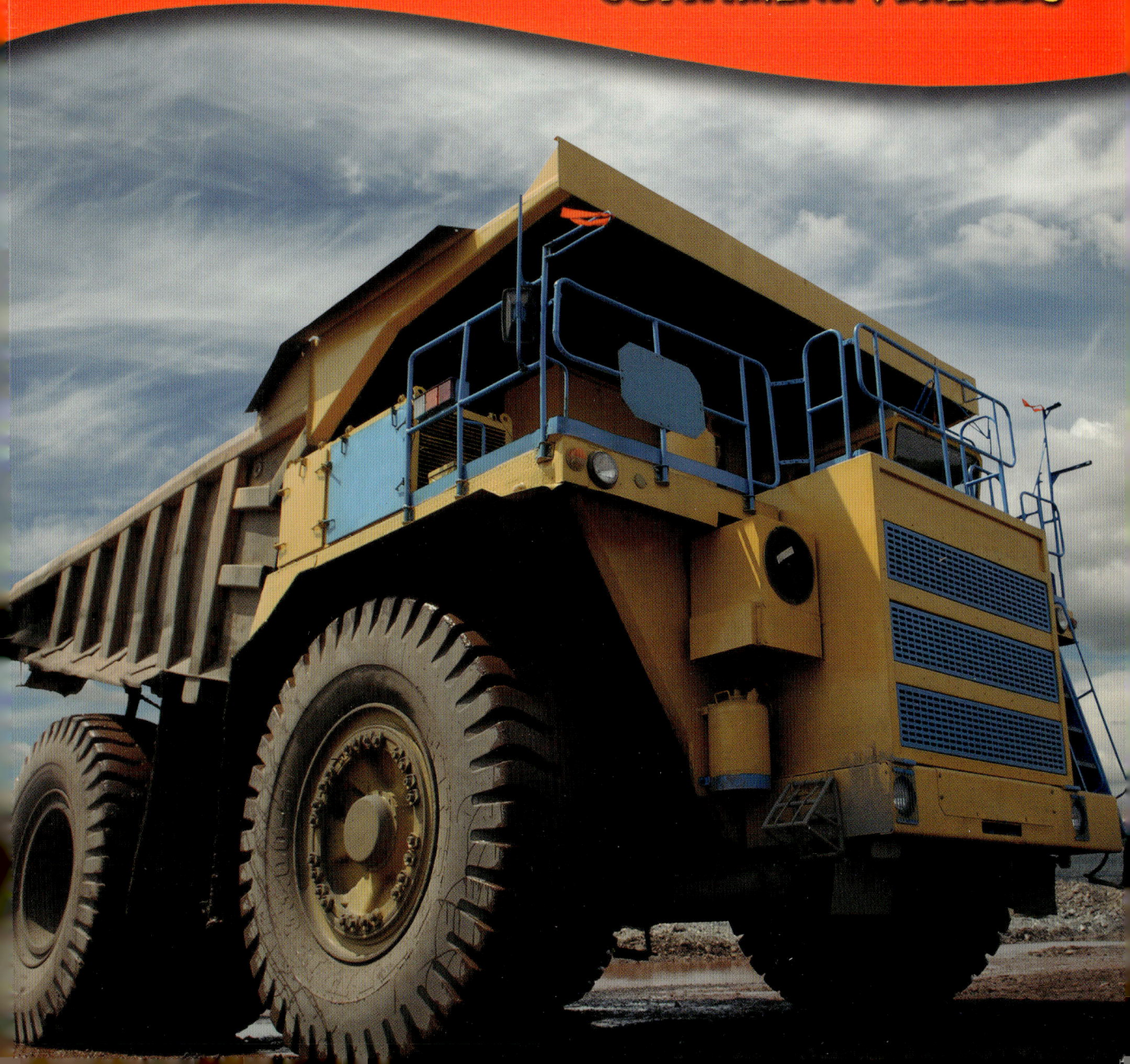

Contents

Measuring weight 4

Why do people build heavy vehicles? 8

Is a toy scooter heavy? 10

Snowmobiles 12

Cars 14

Hot air balloons 16

Fire engines 18

Lorries 20

Jet planes 22

The world's heaviest vehicles 24

Measuring activity 26

Heavy quiz and facts 28

Glossary 30

Find out more 31

Index 32

Words appearing in the text in bold, **like this**,
are explained in the glossary.

Measuring weight

The weight of something is how heavy or light it is. We measure small weights in grams (g), larger weights in kilograms (kg), and really big weights in tonnes (t).

Heavy things are harder to lift.

4

To measure something's weight we can use scales. When you put an object in a **spring scale**, reading the scale will tell you how much the object weighs.

In a supermarket we often use a spring scale to weigh fruit and vegetables.

We can also weigh things by using a **balance scale**. A balance scale has two sides. You put the object to be weighed on one side of the scale and numbered weights on the other side.

The beads weigh more, so the scales have tipped to one side.

If something weighs more on one side, the scales will tip. The scales will balance when the things on both sides weigh the same.

350 grams

When the two sides of the scales balance, the weights tell you how heavy the object is.

Why do people build heavy vehicles?

A vehicle carries people or goods from place to place. Some vehicles are built light. This often makes them fast. For instance, a **motocross** bike is built light, to whizz one rider along in a race.

A light motocross bike can weigh about 91 kilograms.

Other vehicles are built big and heavy, to make them comfortable or to carry heavy loads. This large motorcycle weighs much more than a motocross bike. It can carry two riders comfortably for long journeys.

A large motorcycle like this can weigh more than four motocross bikes.

Is a toy scooter heavy?

Have you ever picked up a toy scooter?
Compared to something like a shoe, it
is heavy. But how heavy is heavy?

A toy scooter can weigh
about 2½ kilograms.

A bicycle is heavier than a toy scooter. An adult's bicycle can weigh around 13½ kilograms. This is about the same as five and a half toy scooters.

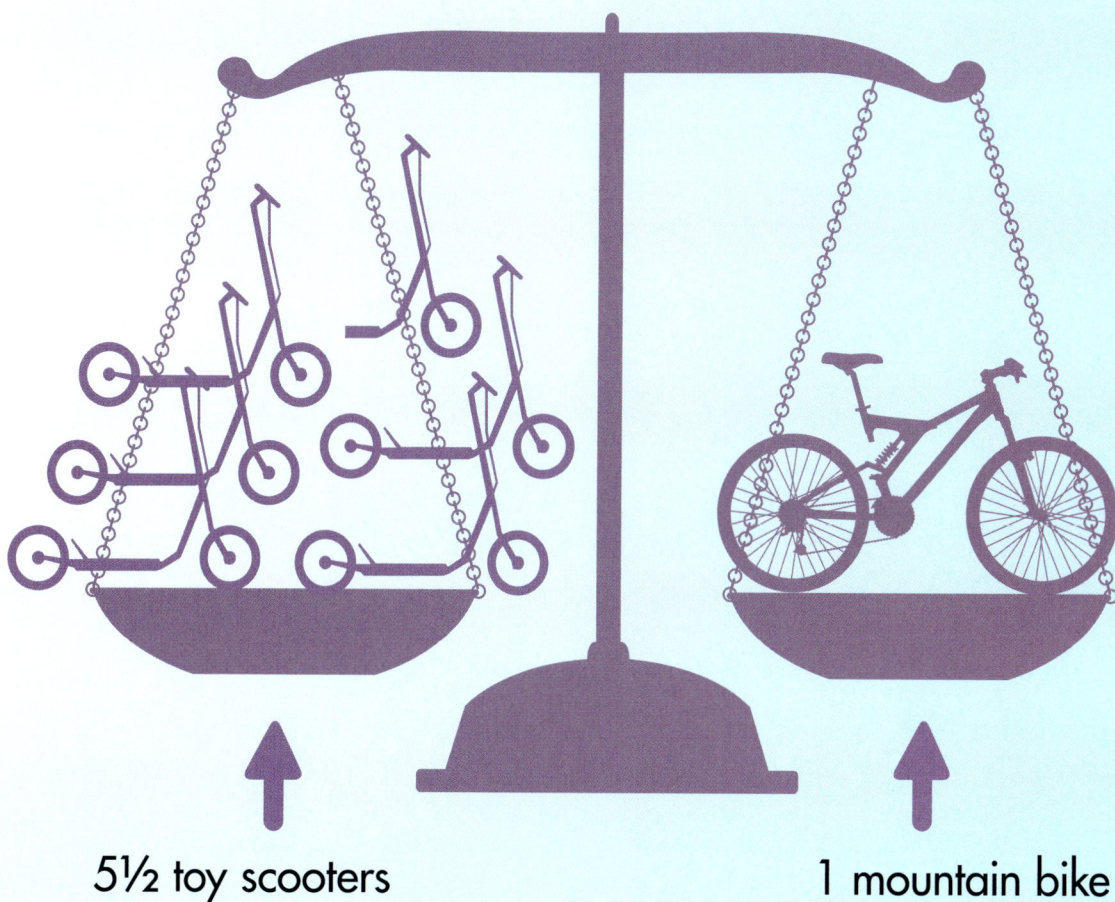

5½ toy scooters

1 mountain bike

What is heavier than a bicycle? ➡

Snowmobiles

A snowmobile is heavier than a bicycle. Snowmobiles are made for speeding anywhere snowy and icy, like mountains – they don't need roads. They are powered by **petrol engines**.

Snowmobiles run on tracks at the back and skis at the front.

A snowmobile like the one in the picture weighs 195 kilograms. This is about the same as 14½ adult bicycles.

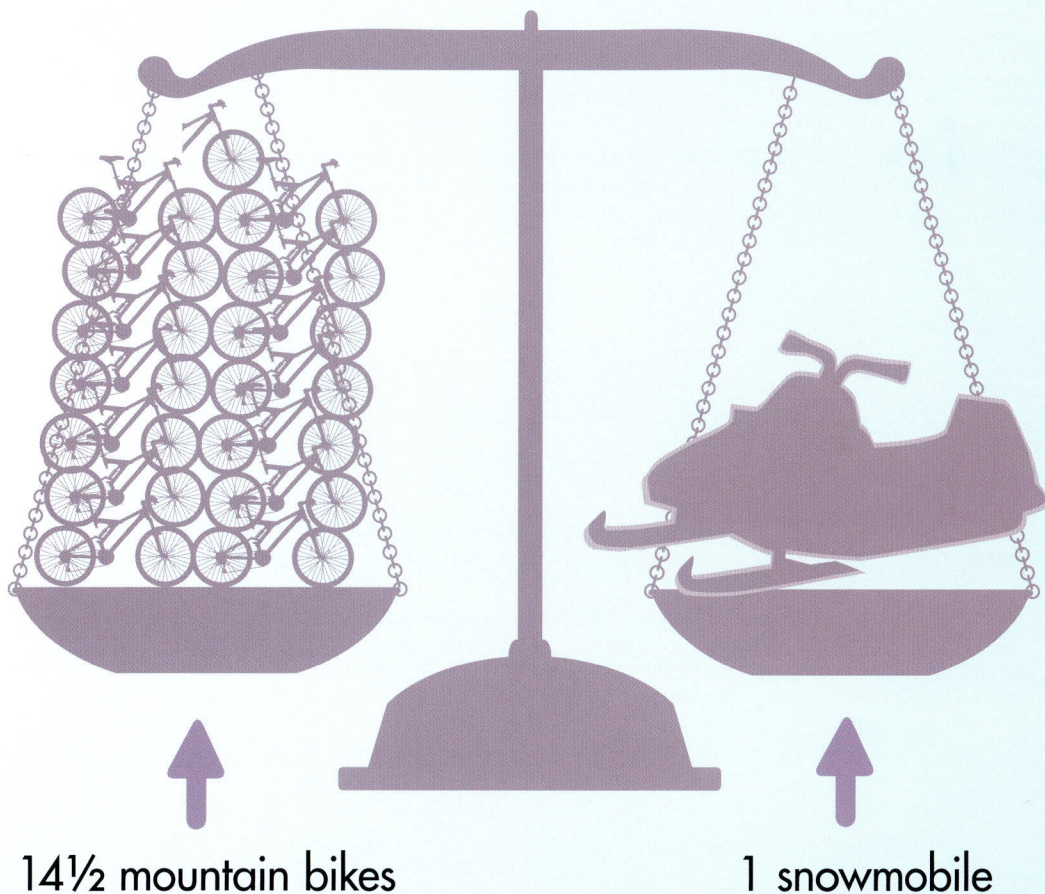

14½ mountain bikes

1 snowmobile

What is heavier than a snowmobile? ➡️

Cars

A car is heavier than a snowmobile. Cars come in many different shapes and sizes, to carry between 1 and 8 passengers. A Mini is one of the smallest cars on the road.

Minis have been made for over 50 years.

A Mini weighs about 1,200 kilograms. This means that a Mini weighs about the same as six snowmobiles put together.

6 snowmobiles   1 Mini

What is heavier than a car? ➡️

Hot air balloons

A hot air balloon is heavier than a car – even though it may not look like it! Hot air balloons can travel very high, glide along quietly, and give their passengers a fantastic view.

These hot air balloons are competing in a race.

An **inflated** hot air balloon for five people can weigh just over 3 tonnes without passengers. It would take about two and a half Minis to weigh as much as this.

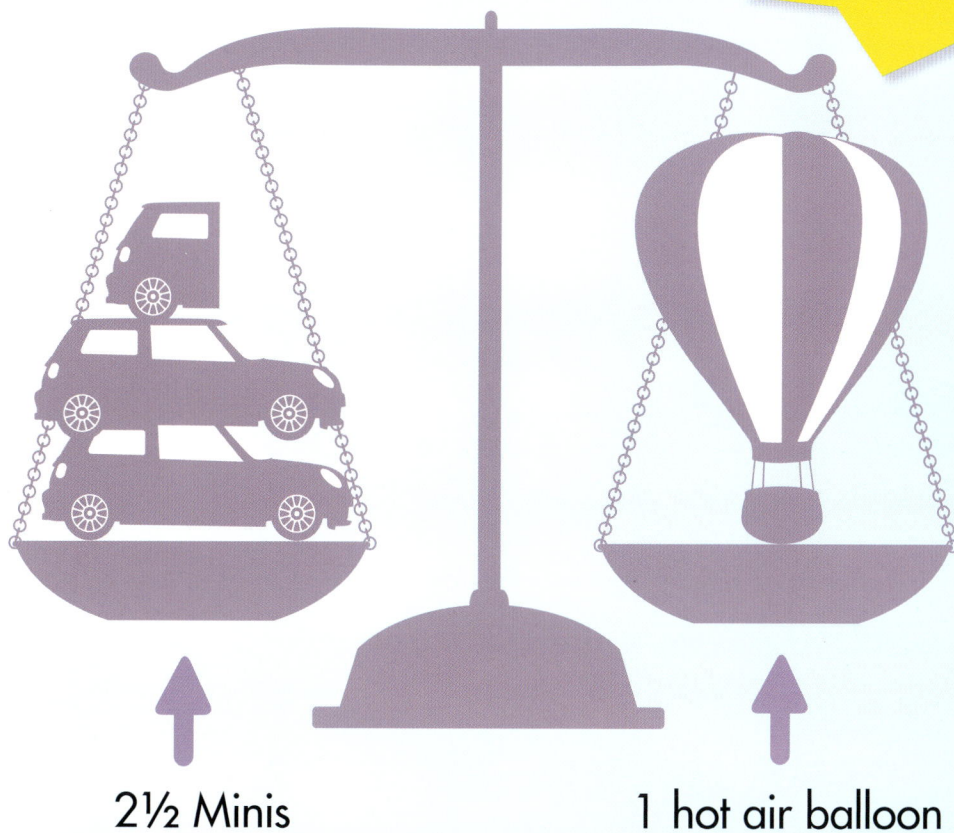

2½ Minis   1 hot air balloon

What is heavier than a hot air balloon? ➡

Fire engines

A fire engine is heavier than a hot air balloon. It has to be big and strong to carry all the fire **crew** and their equipment. The biggest fire engines need 8 wheels or more to support and move their heavy loads.

Fire engines carry huge folding ladders and enormous water hoses.

Many fire engines weigh about 18 tonnes, without their crew. It would take about six hot air balloons to weigh the same as this fire engine.

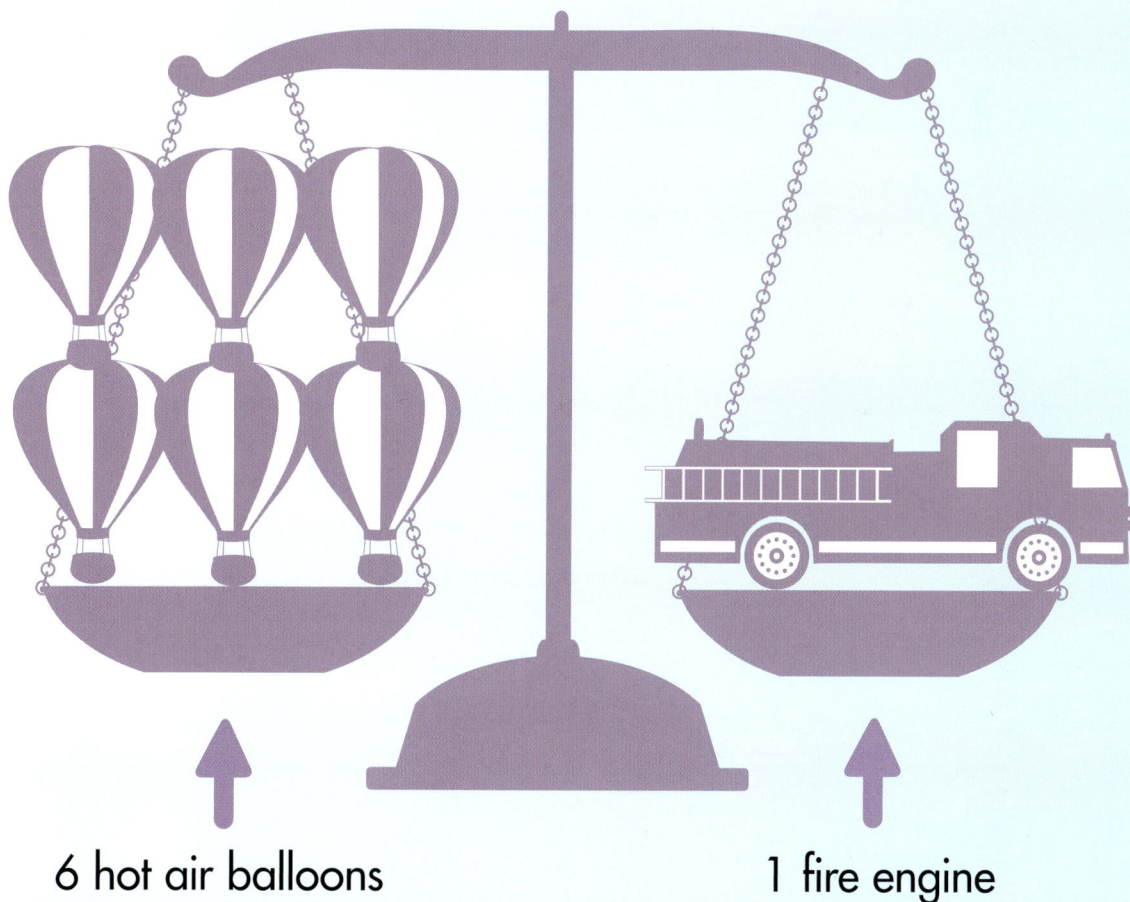

6 hot air balloons

1 fire engine

What is heavier than a fire engine? ➡

Lorries

A lorry can be heavier than a fire engine. The heaviest lorries are called road trains. These are used in some parts of the world to move massive loads.

This type of road train is known as a double.

Even without its load, a double road train can weigh around 83 tonnes. The weight of an unloaded double road train is about the same as four and a half unmanned fire engines.

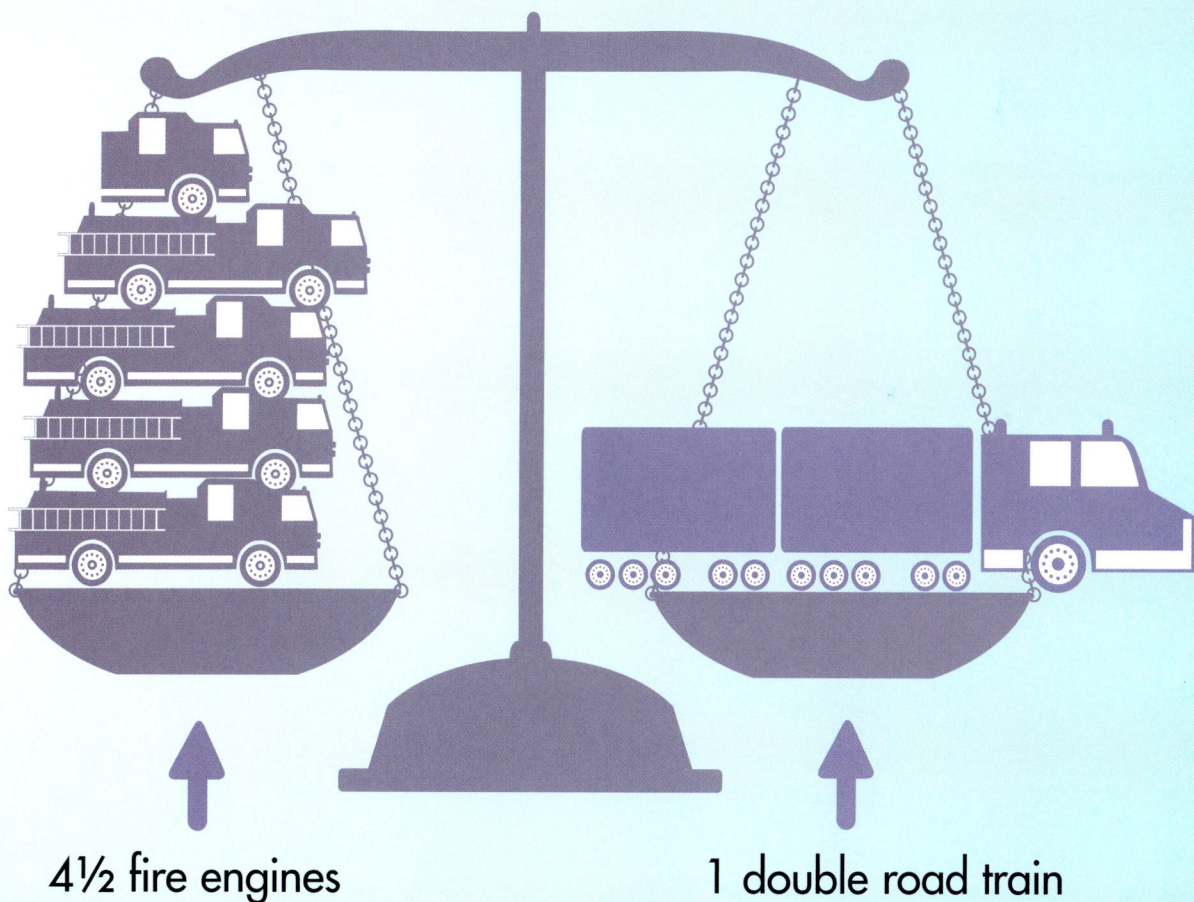

4½ fire engines

1 double road train

What is heavier than a lorry?

Jet planes

A jet plane is heavier than a lorry. Jet planes are the fastest passenger vehicles in the world. This photograph shows a Boeing 747 jet plane.

A Boeing 747 can carry hundreds of people.

An unloaded Boeing 747 jet plane weighs around 162 tonnes. This is nearly as heavy as two unloaded double road trains put together!

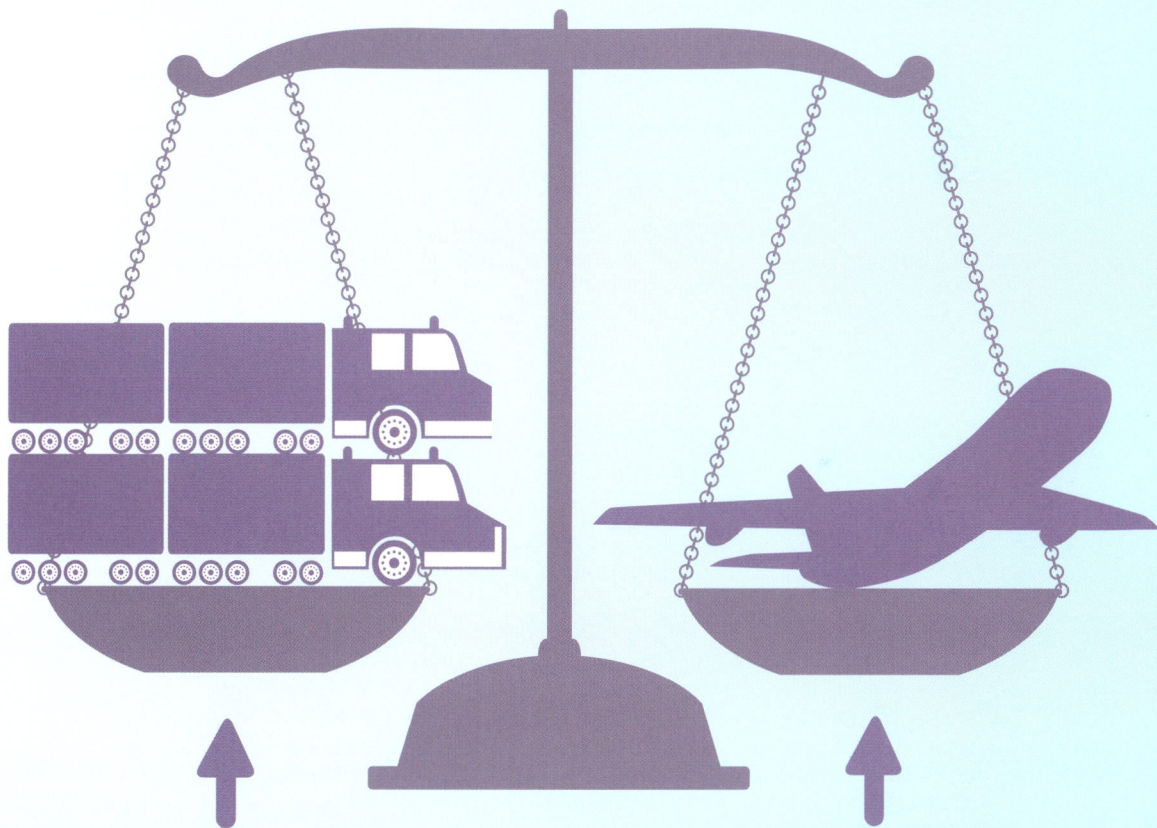

just less than 2 double road trains

1 Boeing 747

What is heavier than a jet plane? ➡

The world's heaviest vehicles

Many ships are heavier than jet planes. Aircraft carriers and cruise ships can be extremely heavy. But supertankers are the heaviest of all.

This cruise ship can carry almost 4,000 people.

The *Knock Nevis* supertanker weighs 564,763 tonnes – unloaded! To weigh the same as the *Knock Nevis* supertanker, it would take nearly 3,478 Boeing jet planes!

This oil tanker, the *Knock Nevis*, is longer than most **skyscrapers** are tall.

Measuring activity

Things you will need: weighing scales, a pencil, paper, and a selection of different-sized objects. Your objects could include: a box of cereal, a pot plant, a metal spoon, a plastic bag, a beach ball, a teacup, a tin of tuna, a plastic cup, and a ping pong ball.

1. Put the objects in a line, starting with the object you think will be the lightest, and ending with the object you think will be the heaviest.

2 Use the scales to weigh all your objects. Write down how much each one weighs.

3 Use your answers to find out if your objects are in the right order.

Find out: Does the weight of an object depend on its size? Are big objects always heavier than smaller objects?

Heavy quiz and facts

Remember

1,000 grams (g) = 1 kilogram (kg)
1,000 kilograms (kg) = 1 tonne (t)

Small weights are measured in grams (g).
Larger weights are measured in kilograms (kg).
Really big weights are measured in tonnes (t).

Quiz

1. What unit would you use to measure the weight of a spaceship?
   a) grams   b) kilograms   c) tonnes

2. What unit would you use to measure the weight of a bicycle?
   a) grams   b) kilograms   c) tonnes

3. What unit would you use to measure the weight of a toy car?
   a) grams   b) kilograms   c) tonnes

Answers: 1 = c   2 = b   3 = a

Heavy facts

- A shire horse can often weigh as much as 910 kilograms.

- An empty Apache helicopter weighs just over 5 tonnes.

- The German Leopard 2 battle tank weighs about 62 tonnes.

- The blue whale is the world's heaviest animal. It can be 172 tonnes or more.

- A massive truck used in mining, called the Liebherr T282B, weighs 237 tonnes.

- Nimitz class warships are the largest type of **aircraft carrier**, called supercarriers. They weigh about 873,000 tonnes when fully loaded.

Glossary

aircraft carrier warship designed to be a floating base for aircraft. It has a long, flat deck on which the aircraft can take off and land.

balance scale tool that measures weight. A balance scale has two sides. When the things put on the two sides of the scales weigh the same, the scales will balance.

crew group of people who work together. The crew on a fire engine are all the firefighters who work on that engine.

cruise ship enormous ship that carries holiday-makers from place to place. It is a bit like a floating hotel, with things such as swimming pools, restaurants, and shops on board.

inflated filled with air

motocross motorcycle race that goes across rough countryside with steep hills and sharp turns

petrol engine machine that turns a fuel called petrol into energy, to make something move

skyscraper extremely tall building for people to live or work in

spring scale tool that measures weight by how much an object pulls down on a spring

Find out more

Books

For Good Measure: The Ways We Say How Much, How Far, How Heavy, How Big, How Old, Ken Robbins (Flash Point, 2010)

My World of Science: Heavy and Light, Angela Royston (Raintree Publishers, 2008)

Start-up Design and Technology: Vehicles, Louise and Richard Spilsbury (Evans Brothers Ltd, 2005)

Websites

www.bbc.co.uk/schools/ks1bitesize/numeracy/measurements/index.shtml

Try measuring the weights on different parcels in the game on this website.

www.bbc.co.uk/skillswise/e3/numbers/measuresshapespace/weight/

Find out about weight through the factsheet, quiz, and weighing scales game on this website.

Index

aircraft carriers 24, 29

balance scale 6–7
battle tanks 29
bicycles 11, 13
blue whales 29
Boeing 747 jet plane 22–23, 25

cars 14–15, 17
cruise ships 24

fire engines 18–19, 21

grams (g) 4, 28

helicopters 29
hot air balloons 16–17, 19

jet planes 22–23, 25

kilograms (kg) 4, 28

lorries 20–21, 23

measuring weight 4–5, 26–27
Minis 14, 15, 17
motocross bikes 8, 9
motorcycles 9

petrol engines 12

road trains 20–21, 23

ships 24–25, 29
shire horses 29
skyscrapers 25
snowmobiles 12–13, 15
spring scale 5
supertankers 24–25

tonnes (t) 4, 28
toy scooters 10–11
trucks 20–21, 23, 29

weight (what it is) 4